What is MAP

(Manufacturing Automation Protocol)?

Colin Pye

PUBLISHED BY NCC PUBLICATIONS

British Library Cataloguing in Publication Data

Pye, Colin
   What is MAP (Manufacturing Automation Protocol)?
   1. Manufacturing industries. Computer systems.
   Protocols. MAP
   I. Title   II. National Computing Centre 670.42′7

ISBN 0-85012-641-X

First published in 1988 by:

NCC Publications, The National Computing Centre Limited, Oxford Road, Manchester M1 7ED, England.

Typeset in 11pt Times Roman by OTS (Typesetting) Services Limited, Chipstead, Surrey; and printed by Hobbs the Printers of Southampton.

ISBN 0-85012-641-X

Acknowledgements

I Would like to thank my colleagues in the Technology Division of NCC for the work that they have put into the MAP programme. Without this work in general and the commitment of NCC in particular, not only to MAP but also to the whole OSI programme, this publication would not have been possible.

In addition I would like to thank my international colleagues on the European User Group OSITOP for their work in furthering the cause of OSI.

Last, but by no means least, I would like to express my thanks to Geoff Simons of NCC for his advice and support of this and other publications, Beverley Martin and Marcia Lamb of NCC for their patience and professionalism, and the NCC typing pool for the speed and accuracy of their work.

Contents

Introduction

This book should be looked upon as putting MAP into perspective, in terms of its origins, the architectural role it is meant to fill in an organisation's communications network hierarchy and the key issues affecting its future development. MAP is a specification, not a standard (although a standard may emerge in the future).

It is a specification which defines the use of international standards; this means (because some standards have not reached full international status) that the specification is still evolving (this has been seen through version releases 1.0, 2.1, 2.2 up to the current 3.0). Each version release marked a significant step in the development of the specification. MAP, conceived by General Motors in the United States, was born out of the need to get incompatible equipment, installed on the factory floor, to communicate cost-effectively. General Motors has done much to promote the needs of the end-user and, whatever the decision in adopting MAP within a specific organisation, one should acknowledge and pay tribute to GM efforts.

Since MAP is based on International Standards the book assumes some knowledge of the Open Systems Interconnection (OSI) concept; however, Chapter 1 gives an overview of the standards and standardisation process. Readers not having knowledge of this area are directed towards the NCC publications *What is OSI?* and *Migrating to OSI*.

This book does not deal with strategic implications or cost justification of adopting MAP — because if 'N' different companies are considered here there will be 'N' different communication network designs leading to 'N' different views on cost justification.

For this reason Chapter 2 deals with the MAP architecture and discusses broadly where MAP could fit.

Chapter 3 deals with the MAP specification. It references the international standards used at each layer without discussing them in detail. It is more important to know the justification and limitations of the international standards used.

Whether or not MAP, or for that matter any other specification trying to achieve what MAP is trying to achieve, is accepted worldwide depends on the user's reaction to it. First and foremost it must satisfy the user's needs: it must be able to provide a technical solution to user's problems and allow the user to invest in new equipment, with the confidence that MAP will continue to be supported and that any equipment bought to the MAP specification will interwork with other manufacturers' equipment. This second point is addressed in Chapter 4 under 'Testing MAP Implementations'. The continued support for MAP is addressed in Chapter 5 (attention to user, vendor and organisational support). The final chapter takes a look at the future.

MAP is based on international standards and follows the concept of Open Systems Interconnection (OSI), put forward by the International Standards Organisation (ISO). MAP is meant to satisfy requirements of manufacturing industry but standards have an impact on all sectors of industry: retailing, banking, etc. OSI can then be thought of as a kernel (as shown in Figure 0.1).

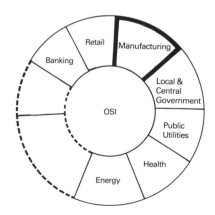

Figure 0.1   The Impact of OSI Related to Business Sectors

There will be variation in requirements for each of the business sectors illustrated. This will be required in 'compliance' testing for various functional profiles (eg MAP, TOP, GOSIP, etc). The uptake of OSI within the manufacturing industry will be felt in organisations' Computer Integrated Manufacturing (CIM) strategies. CIM relates to integrating a company's functions. Although this book does not address CIM, it is important to understand that MAP cannot purely relate to shop-floor communications: it is no good manufacturing a product more efficiently if there is no control on the invoicing of the raw materials, supplying post manufactured documentation, etc. In this respect it should be stressed that any organisation contemplating using MAP within their CIM strategy should ensure that other strategies (for example, voice, office systems, data — globally termed 'Information Technology' strategies) are taken into account. This may seem obvious but often voice communication networks evolve with no consideration given to data requirements, and vice versa!

The problems of bringing together the various requirements of finance, manufacturing, sales, marketing, etc are dealt with briefly in Chapter 2.

The appendices comprise a glossary of commonly used terms and a list of the standards laid down within the MAP specification. The final appendix can be used by the reader as a source of reference in addition to his own local MAP User Group. The fact that large companies grow by acquisition as well as by internal growth, underlines the fact that communications is a board-level subject and thus a major part of a company's business plan. Imagine the disastrous consequences if a recently acquired company was not able to provide the relevant interfaces with which to interwork with its new partner.

1 Standards and Standardisation

INTRODUCTION

As a basic philosophy, MAP adheres to the International Standards Organisation (ISO) reference model for Open Systems Interconnection (OSI). This chapter gives a brief overview of that model, including its structure and the functions it is meant to perform. The reference model is fundamental to understanding what MAP is trying to achieve. The chapter sets the scene to help the reader to understand some of the decisions that went into developing the MAP specification.

COMMUNICATION STANDARDS

MAP is one example of the use of data communication standards to solve a particular problem – that of interconnecting incompatible equipments intended for use in manufacturing systems. It has assumed particular importance because it uses the concept of Open Systems Interconnection (OSI) rather than relying on proprietary solutions. It was specified from the outset that MAP would, where possible, use current or emerging OSI standards and would adopt the basic reference model as its framework. Because MAP is based on OSI it is necessary to look at the OSI architecture in order to appreciate fully what MAP is trying to achieve.

The standardisation process is a major undertaking which has been in progress for over ten years (see *What is OSI?*, NCC, 1988). Existing standards are very complex and indeed some are still being developed. This meant that through the evolution of the MAP specification some intercepts had to be specified by the MAP taskforce and some interim solutions defined as the specification evolved. Nevertheless, MAP is based on an architectural model.

THE ARCHITECTURAL MODEL

The architectural model defines a logical structure whereby the functions required for the communications process can take place. In order to communicate effectively it is necessary to have a predefined set of rules so that both parties are able to understand when they can transmit information and when they can receive it. For this purpose, use is made of *protocols*. Before looking at communications architectures it is necessary to indicate the characteristics of a protocol.

A protocol is essentially an agreement between two partners to use a common set of rules in order to exchange information. When the partners are computers or any other equipment using programmable devices they can only follow a set of unambiguous instructions; hence it is necessary to strictly define the protocol rules. Protocols for communications specify rules for:

— transmission speed;

— format of data;

— handling transmission errors;

— addressing rules;

— data interpretation.

There are many other rules regarding protocols but these are some of the basic requirements. The arrangement of the protocols into an order which is useable is the basis of a communications architecture. In order to get two pieces of equipment to 'talk' to each other, protocols must be:

— processing oriented;

— communications oriented.

The processing-oriented protocols are those which are associated with the applications and characteristics of the end-user equipment. The purpose of the communications-oriented protocols is to ensure that the data arrives at its destination correctly and efficiently using the appropriate transmission media (see Figure 1.1).

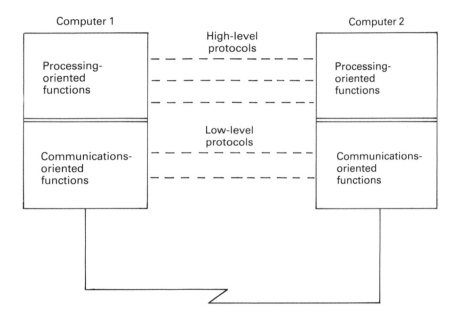

Figure 1.1   Processing-oriented and Communications-oriented Protocols

Communications-oriented protocols received the earliest attention. Many computer manufacturers who designed their own proprietary systems also designed their own proprietary data transmission protocols. This made interworking between different manufacturers' equipment difficult, and in most cases impossible; and in some instances it made interworking between the manufacturers' own equipment impossible because incompatible data transmission protocols had been defined to serve different applications on their own systems. The most significant advance in the standardisation of protocols in order to achieve independence of the internal format of the data held in the computers was the High Level Data Link Control (HDLC) protocol. This protocol is now a basic requirement for most data transmission protocols which are used within the computer and communications industry.

HDLC did have limitations in that it was intended for use over a single circuit joining the source and destination end users. A large number of computer communications systems, both public and private, use networks which require the interconnection of a large number of devices. In order to achieve this interconnection a more complex protocol was required. This ensured that data arrived error free, and that in a complex network having many different routes between end systems the correct routes were chosen. The CCITT developed a protocol called X.25 which was designed specifically to cope with these large networks. The protocol defines three distinct levels:

Level 1   —   defines the interface to the physical medium

Level 2   —   defines the control of the data over the link into the network (this is based on HDLC)

Level 3   —   defines the format and meaning of the data contained in the HDLC frames, the network addressing, the route management, etc.

X.25 thus defines the communications-oriented functions required for a protocol. These functions, sub-divided into the levels explained above, can be used to define the basic requirements for a communications architecture. The requirements for a communications architecture defined within X.25 can be mapped onto a general architectural requirement having identified key points which must be included in any communications architecture.

In a similar fashion the processing-oriented functions will also provide a set of protocols, each one using the services provided by those below it, which can be used to define the key points necessary for protocols required to satisfy processing-oriented functions. This arrangement of the protocols and the services into a predefined hierarchy is most commonly called a communications or network architecture. The mapping of the communications-oriented functions and the processing-oriented functions onto this architecture is shown in Figure 1.2.

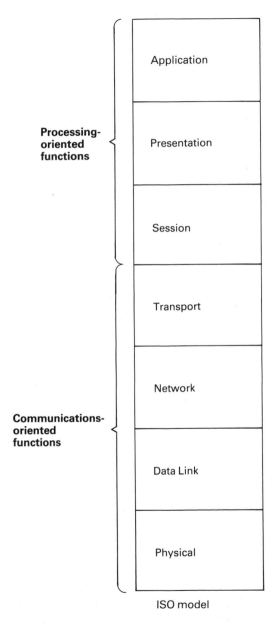

Figure 1.2 Mapping of Functions onto ISO Model

The great advantage in defining an architecture of this type is that it breaks down the complex tasks required in communications into more easily understandable and handled subtasks. The relationship between these tasks can then be defined in terms of the service each task expects of the task below, the facilities each task offers to the one immediately above, and the interfaces between the various tasks. An architecture has limitations in that it defines neither how each protocol is implemented nor its mode of operation. It merely helps the computer and communications designers to identify the various functions and place them in hardware or software without specifying which is the preferred solution.

Communications architectures are not a new concept; indeed each computer manufacturer has historically defined his own architecture. Unfortunately, because each is defined by individual computer manufacturers within their own discrete environments, the architectures are incompatible. The Open Systems Interconnection architecture resulted through collaboration between the users and suppliers. The aim was to design a standard architecture which would have the required functionality and, because it was a consensus process, the generality to be adopted by everyone. The value of the architecture is in the fact that the subtasks and protocols can be defined so that compatibility between different systems is assured. It is this which is the aim of OSI.

OSI addresses the problem of incompatible equipment. A framework is proposed whereby manufacturers who adhere to the standards laid down within the OSI concept will more easily be able to achieve interworking between their equipments. OSI does not merely involve the design and standardisation of the architecture but also includes the protocols and required services which are meant to fit within the OSI framework in order to provide the means for data exchange. Before introducing the OSI reference model in more detail, it is worthwhile examining local area network (LAN) standards as these play a crucial role in the MAP specification.

LOCAL AREA NETWORKS STANDARDS

The IEEE did much of the initial work in defining the standards for local area networks. This has now been taken up within the International Standards Organisation in order to enable the standards to evolve up to full international status. The IEEE defined the local area network standardisation work as Project No. 802. This means that the various local area network standards defined by the IEEE are called 802.X, where X is used to define the type of local area network covered by the standard. Corresponding ISO standards to those defined by IEEE are numbered 8802/X, where X corresponds to the IEEE suffix. The following projects are of particular relevance:

IEEE 802.1   –   LAN Higher Layer Protocols, Systems Management and Internetworking

IEEE 802.2   –   Logical Link Control, Data Link Functions which are independent of the physical medium used

IEEE 802.3   –   Carrier Sense Multiple Access with Collision Detect (CSMA/CD)

IEEE 802.4   –   Token Passing Bus

IEEE 802.5   –   Token Passing Ring

IEEE 802.3, 802.4 and 802.5 (those associated with media access) all extend over more than one OSI layer – the physical and data link layers. These are called Medium Access Control (MAC) standards and define the ways of attaching and using the appropriate medium, resolving contention, signalling methods, etc. IEEE 802.2 defines Media Independent Datalink Functions and interfaces to the MAC specifications in order to complete the datalink layer service. Figure 1.3 shows the relationship of IEEE 802 standards and the way that they fit in within the OSI model. This model can now be described in more detail.

THE OSI REFERENCE MODEL

The model is the International Standards Organisation (ISO) reference model for Open Systems Interconnection (OSI) and defines the framework within which the standards for OSI can be developed in order to achieve freedom of interconnection between the different suppliers of computer and communications equipment.

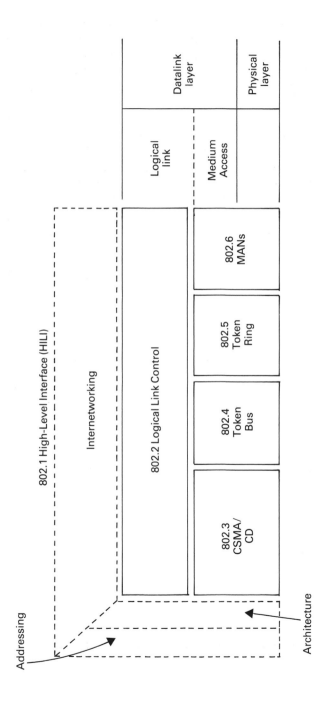

Figure 1.3   Interrelationship Between IEEE LAN Standards

The model itself comprises seven layers (see Figure 1.4). It is the responsibility of each layer to define a specific function or group of functions which can be handled together; however, all seven layers will be implemented in the systems which ultimately send and receive information. Open Systems Interconnection does not define the characteristics of the physical medium or network of media used during this interconnection. In the same respect the applications programs which the end users will want to use on their systems are outside the scope of the reference model, the application layer only providing services to the application programs. As shown in Figure 1.4, protocols defined for each layer of the model may only communicate with their peer level protocols in other systems — peer to peer protocols. It is a basic rule that no OSI layer protocol is allowed to communicate with another layer in another system.

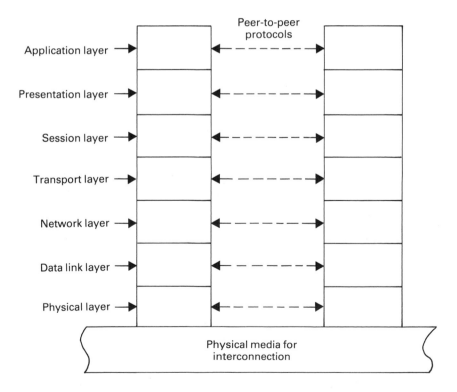

Figure 1.4   ISO Seven-layer Reference Model

Due to the fact that each protocol may only communicate with its peer level protocol in an often remote end system, it is necessary that all communications must be routed down through the layers, across the communications medium, and up through the layers of the remote end system. It is this requirement which defines yet another characteristic of the model: each layer must offer a service to the layer immediately above it and expect a service from the layers below. Each defined layer protocol is thus the means by which that particular layer provides the service (see Figure 1.5). It can be concluded therefore that in defining each layer there must be at least two standards, one for the service definition and the other for the protocol definition. As the model was reached through consensus, each layer in fact has a range of optional standards within it.

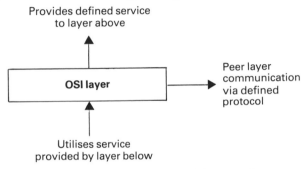

Figure 1.5   Services and Protocols

Of the seven layers of the basic reference model, the top three are concerned with the processing-oriented functions, the lower four with the communications-oriented functions. The three lower layers use protocols which will be tailored to the actual physical media being used. It is easy to envisage a situation in a large network whereby information being transmitted from one end user to another will require several hops between these end systems. It is also entirely feasible that the various hops will use different physical media. Thus there is a requirement for relay devices to be defined in order to handle the interfaces between the networks. The relays implement only layers 1, 2 and 3 − the media-dependent layers. Layer 4, the transport layer, is a communications-oriented function which implements a protocol operating between 2 end systems, independent of the media used. Figure 1.6 gives an example of the use of a relay device.

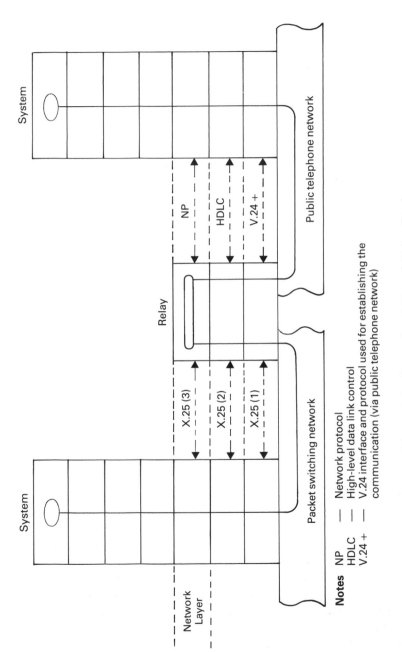

Figure 1.6 Example of Use of Relay Device

MAP is not purely concerned with local area networks; it also has a requirement to define interfaces with wide area networks (WAN). The original reference model defined a network which required each system that would be involved in the transfer of information to establish a liaison before any information could be exchanged. This was referred to as a connections-oriented system. It was later recognised that not all applications or networks fall into this category and it was necessary to amend the reference model and cater for those situations in which no prior agreement is reached before information is transmitted − the connectionless service. There are no rules to say that this must apply at all levels: a local area network may involve a connectionless service in the lower layers but the applications may operate as though a permanent connection has been set up in a connections-oriented manner.

The basic reference model envisaged the major requirements for intercommunication to be between computer-based systems. The further complexity and evolution of communication networks has required extensions to the original model, covering such items as:

— network management;

— naming and addressing;

— security.

It is now a good time to turn to the basic reference model and examine it layer by layer.

Physical Layer

The physical layer (layer 1 in the OSI Reference Model) is the lowest defined layer. It specifies the interface to the physical medium used. However, it does not specify how the medium or network transports the actual information. An example of this could be that the physical medium used could relate to the public switched telephone network (PSTN) or private circuit. In another of the defined cases, the physical layer controls the interface circuits to the modem which is in itself part of the physical medium. The standard also defines part of the data link layer functions which are dependent on the actual physical medium and access method used. These are concerned with the techniques for sharing the local area network transmission media, ie resolving contention, handling of tokens and frequency band allocation. In this way, the local area network standards which are media dependent are called the medium access control (MAC) specifications. With respect to wide area networks, there are similarly a large number of options for the physical layer which relate to the various possible network characteristics.

The Datalink Layer

No matter which physical data transmission medium is used, it will give random errors during the process of data transmission. This is still likely to occur even though local area networks and digital circuits are less likely to introduce errors than are previous methods. The purpose of the data link layer is to recognise this fact and minimise the number of errors passed on to the layers above by defining some of its functions in such a way as to handle this requirement. This is achieved by setting up the data into recognisable frames detecting, and where possible correcting, errors which have been introduced by the physical medium during the transmission process. It is a requirement of this layer that it should support a connections-oriented or connectionless mode of operation. Local area networks would normally use connectionless mode of transmission and for this type of service true error correction is not possible. However, errors may be detected and, without being corrected, flagged up to the layer above − the network layer. It is then the responsibility of the network layer to decide what action should be taken. The logical link control (LLC) sublayer defines two types of service:

— connectionless oriented (type 1);

— connection oriented (type 2).

Two classes of service are also specified:

— that which supports type 1 operation only (class 1);

— that which supports both types of operation (class 2).

The medium access control local area network standards implement the whole of the physical layer and part of the data link layer concerned with gaining access to the medium. The IEEE 802.2 stan-

dard completes the data link layer and provides the correct interface to the network layer.

The Network Layer

This layer performs the addressing and routeing functions needed
to transport messages between the end systems involved. If several
subnetworks are involved, each with its own naming and addressing structures, this can result in a complex task. Like those layers
below it, the network layer is partially dependent on the actual
physical medium or network in use. This means that a different
implementation is required for each of the separate subnetworks
which go to form the whole network providing the interconnection
between the two end systems. If the subnetworks themselves cannot provide an OSI service they have to be enhanced so that the
interface to the transport layer is what is expected. The network
layer, in providing the interconnection function for the subnetworks,
interconnects each subnetwork by means of relay systems as
illustrated in Figure 1.6. Each relay specified within the overall interconnection acts as a gateway between different subnetworks and
so must be able to implement the network, datalink and physical
layer functions relevant to each subnetwork. The layer above the
network layer is the transport layer.

The Transport Layer

In OSI it is the responsibility of the transport layer to provide a
service which is independent of the physical media or networks
employed. It provides end-to-end transmission of information across
the network. The transport layer supports both connections-oriented
and connectionless transmission. However, before any communications can take place between end systems in a connectionless mode
they must previously agree a common transport protocol. With
respect to systems involved in a connections-oriented transfer, the
protocol agreement can take place during a negotiation phase prior
to the exchange of data.

When a connections-oriented network layer service is employed,
the transport layer currently defines five communications protocols
(classes) of differing characteristics:

Class 0 – A simple class, no enhancement to the network service

Class 1 – Basic Error Recovery Class

Class 2 – Multiplexing Class

Class 3 – Error Recovery and Multiplexing

Class 4 – Error Detection and Recovery Class

For the multiple transport connections the transport layer can use a single network connection (ie a real or virtual circuit). This means that one network connection can support a number of simultaneous interactions. In addition, the transport connection can also use network connections in parallel in order to provide a level of service which would otherwise be impossible with a single network connection – hence the need for multiplexing classes in the transport protocol. Error recovery options stated within the transport classes relate to the capabilities of the network and media used, ie those with poor facilities will require enhancement at the transport layer.

The remaining three layers – the first being the session layer – are now concerned with processing oriented functions.

The Session Layer

This layer supports the establishment control and termination of information exchanges between end users or application programs. In addition it also supports activities such as synchronisation, checkpointing and re-establishment of connections, should a failure occur. The session service implements the following functions:

— normal data exchange;

— expedited data exchange: data may overtake data being transferred using normal data exchange;

— token management: used to control other services;

— dialogue control: two-way alternate or two-way simultaneous data exchange;

—   synchronisation: the insertion of marks into the data stream in order to synchronise;

—   re-synchronisation: in order to restart the data transfer;

—   activity management: in order to divide dialogue into separately managed activities;

—   exception reporting: in order to notify errors and other unexpected events;

—   typed data: to allow a session to send transparent user data;

—   capability data: to allow a session to send a limited amount of user data.

The session protocol required to implement the above listed functions contains several optional features which are grouped into 'functional units'. The presentation layer requirements influence the choice of the subsets of these options which are:

—   session kernel: always required and includes services to set up and terminate connections and transfer data;

—   basic combined subset: the smallest session subset comprising session kernel and half and full-duplex dialogue control;

—   basic synchronised subset: provides limited user control and comprises session kernel, dialogue control, synchronisation, typed data and negotiated release;

—   basic activity subset: allows user interaction and consists of session kernel, half-duplex, typed data, some synchronisation, activity management, exception reporting and capability data exchange;

—   basic activity subset: provides support for CCITT message handling service and comprises session kernel, half and full-duplex, typed data, full synchronisation and activity management.

The layer above the session layer is the presentation layer which is responsible for 'presenting' the information to the application layer, applications programs or end-users in a format which they are able to understand.

The Presentation Layer

The presentation layer provides much of the device independence required of open systems interconnection. It is concerned only with the syntax of the data (the application layer being responsible for its interpretation and hence its meaning). In order to provide this service a number of presentation layer functions have been defined:

— session establishment and termination requests;

— data transfer;

— negotiation and renegotiation of syntax;

— the transformation of syntax including data transformation, formatting and special transformations; for example, data compression.

The Application Layer

This is the highest layer defined in the OSI reference model and provides the services to support the applications and end users who need to communicate with others using an OSI system. It is inaptly named since the application layer provides services to the application programs and does not contain any application programs itself, although some application systems and indeed packages may implement the appropriate application layer services as part of themselves. The structure of the application layer is shown in Figure 1.7, while the components are listed below (however, some changes are currently taking place — see ACSE in the glossary of terms):

— specific application service element (SASE): the services which serve users or applications directly, eg file transfer access and management (FTAM) service, virtual terminal service, job transfer and manipulation service;

— common application service elements (CASE): services required by all application processors and other application services, eg to set up and terminate a connection;

— user-specific service elements: services required for specific applications and groups of users within a common application, eg airlines, banks.

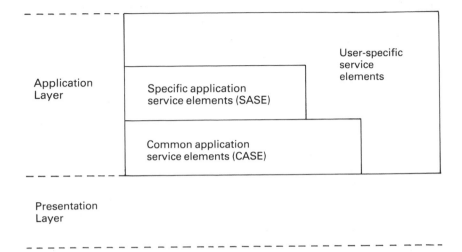

Figure 1.7   Structure of the Application Layer

CONCLUSION

Open systems interconnection is still under development; however, the basic reference model is an international standard (IS), as are some of the services and protocols for the layers. Many of the standards are in draft international standard (DIS), draft proposal (DP) or working paper (WP) form. This means that the number of options open to users specifying protocol stacks for particular applications is increasing. Within each layer there are potentially several options to choose from. This means that systems implementing OSI must have chosen not only the same network but also the same or at least compatible options in each layer if they are to exchange meaningful information.

It is now becoming more common to choose groups of protocols which together define a route through the open systems model from layers 1 through to 7 and which meet a particular requirement. These groups or subsets of protocols are called protocol stacks and define the options to be implemented at each specific layer. Usually only one protocol is chosen for each layer. However, in the application layer more than one may be needed to provide the support required for all of the applications and end users. MAP is actually one of these stacks of protocols falling within the OSI architecture. From the outset, General Motors decided to base MAP on international standards where appropriate. However, during MAP's evolution it was found that suitable standards in some cases did not exist. When this was the case, General Motors decided to define interim standards with the objective of migrating to international standards when they became available. General Motors, in specifying that MAP should adhere to international standards, has done a great deal to further the advancement and indeed accelerate the acceptance of open systems interconnection concepts by end-users, not just in the manufacturing sector but in all other sectors (retail, banking, etc). The users within these sectors are now beginning to understand the potential of open systems interconnection as applicable within their own specific environments. We are now entering a phase in all sectors of industry whereby open systems interconnection will become an integral part of a company's business strategy.

2 MAP Architecture

INTRODUCTION

Chapter 1 explained the concept of the International Standards Organisation (ISO) model for Open Systems Interconnection (OSI), and explained that it was this model upon which MAP is architecturally based. For open systems interconnection to function as primarily envisaged, the layers implemented in each of the interconnected nodes must correspond exactly. This means that if node A needs to interchange information with node B then all seven layers present in node A must correspond to the seven layers present in node B and provide the same functionality. In the current manufacturing environment this becomes restrictive mainly because of the fact that the systems already in place and implemented within an overall communications hierarchy are proprietary from a number of different manufacturers.

General Motors has stated that the intent of the Manufacturing Automation Protocol specification is to establish the requirements for factory local area networks to support communication among computers and other intelligent devices. GM have also stated that, with recent appropriation requests for plant floor computer systems, as much as 50% of the total funding has been allocated to device interconnection and communications. The objective of MAP therefore is to define a specification using current or emerging standards which can be implemented in all varieties of computers, terminals and programmable devices. The MAP specification does not stop at defining requirements for local area networks; it also impacts on wide area network requirements (and in doing so must deal with the needs of finance, manufacturing, sales and marketing departments). MAP defines a number of architectural building blocks, the purpose of which is explained within this chapter. Fundamental common ground in getting different incompatible devices to communicate with each other is that the cabling connection, at the physical medium itself, must be accessible from all parts of the shop-floor and make itself available for use by other factory departments.

There are practical limitations to the route which the cable can take across the shop floor:

— the inherent flexibility of the cable may restrict access through certain ducts;

— the routeing of the cable across the shop floor or within the plant may be restricted through security considerations;

— routeing may be restricted so that the cable is accessible, taking into account maintenance considerations;

— future planning of plant layout should play a part in cable routeing.

In addition to considering the practical aspects of installation of the cable and the geographical limitations, network restrictions must also take account of:

— ability of the network to meet the design and performance criteria;

— requirements to individually manage sections of the network;

— connection to none MAP (proprietary) systems in the local area and wide area context.

The MAP specification allows for these situations by defining the building blocks referred to previously in terms of their architectural and functional attributes. These building blocks are then used to interconnect various subnetworks and comprise:

— backbone architecture (MAP end systems);

— cell architecture;

— MAP system architecture;

— MAP router;

— MAP bridge;

— MAP gateway;

— MAP/EPA system;

— mini MAP system.

THE BACKBONE ARCHITECTURE (MAP END SYSTEMS)

The most common implementation of a MAP network will involve a broader backbone with nodes connected to that backbone or dropped to each of the connected devices as illustrated in Figure 2.1. The backbone itself may be linear or branched, so being suitable for a wide variety of systems such as distributed control systems, shop-floor data collection systems or equipment on flexible production lines. A backbone architecture itself uses the IEEE 802.4 broadband token bus as stated in the MAP specification (see Chapter 3). Its main function is to be the mainstay of the MAP network on the factory floor and to interconnect MAP end systems.

MAP end systems are nodes on the network which contain an implementation of the full seven layers of the MAP architecture. They will communicate with each other through peer-to-peer communications as specified in the open systems interconnection model discussed in Chapter 1. The MAP backbone network is meant to run over long lengths throughout the factory floor. It is meant to bring together shop-floor systems, proprietary gateways and subnetworks. The subnetworks themselves are used to connect cells of programmable controllers or intelligent devices and will typically comprise less than 30 nodes and under 2000 metres in length. This then gives some idea of the geographical dimensions that the backbone network was meant to span. In summary, MAP end systems and their functions can be defined as:

— comprising a stack of OSI protocols for layers 1 to 7 as defined in the MAP specification;

— able to communicate with other end systems on a peer-to-peer basis either on the local MAP subnetwork or at a remote site via an intermediate OSI network;

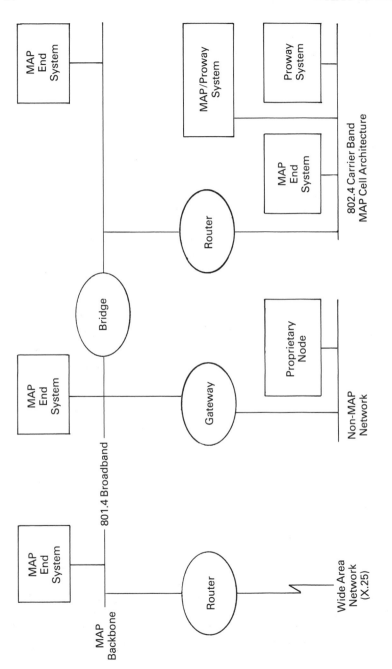

Figure 2.1 MAP Architecture

— able to cater for the use of alternative physical layers (broad-band or carrier band) (see Chapter 3).

THE MAP CELL ARCHITECTURE

It was recognised that many manufacturing installations in the future will continue to be configured as linked cells. The configuration of such cells could be defined by machine-related functions (all machines of the same type within the same geographical area) or product-related (all machines required to make an end product linked within the same geographical area). Whichever configuration is chosen the control of the manufacturing process will require communications between the supervisory systems and the individual cells so that management and production control information can be kept up-to-date and hence maximising throughput and minimising downtime.

Existing installations, and indeed any new installations, will undoubtedly utilise equipment from single suppliers: such as TIWAY, MODBUS, and Data Highway from Texas, Gould and Allen Bradley respectively. The MAP cell architecture takes this into account but proposes to rationalise the situation through the use of carrier band, MAP/PROWAY systems and PROWAY systems to complete the total network architecture. To summarise, the communications network selected for this level must take account of:

— the geographical distribution of devices;

— the flexibility and reconfiguration requirements of the system;

— response time requirements;

— existing installed communications systems.

Many of the low-cost time critical requirements which are present in the manufacturing industry are also present in the process control industry and it is this fact which is giving an extra push to achieving solutions at the cell level which are also applicable to control systems. It is for this reason that 'cut down' versions of MAP have been specified in order to improve response times and reduce costs.

THE MAP SYSTEM ARCHITECTURE

MAP does not limit itself to a definition of local area requirements. The MAP architecture comprises the backbone architecture, cell architecture and other required devices which will provide interconnection to MAP systems and non-MAP systems within the local area network environment and wide area network environment. The architecture encompasses the overall corporate network design (see Figure 2.2). It can be concluded from studying Figure 2.2 that MAP clearly has an impact on equipment procurement which reaches far beyond pure manufacturing data requirements of an organisation (this point is discussed in Chapter 6).

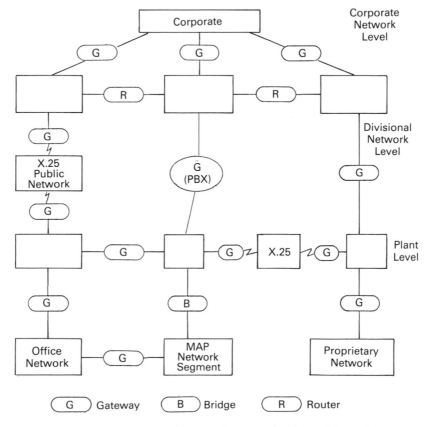

Figure 2.2 Example of a Communications Hierarchy

THE MAP ROUTER

The layered architecture of the MAP router is shown in Figure 2.3.
It will be used to connect several networks together at a common
point and provide path selection and alternative routeing based on
the destination network layer addresses and status of the connected
networks. The router has a single common network address for all
the attached networks while the dissimilar subnetworks are joined
by the router using the ISO Internet network protocol. The subnetworks themselves may operate independently, having different data
link protocols (eg X.25), independently assigned station addresses,
different restrictions concerning their own operation (eg packet size,
speed, priorities). In addition they may also have several different
physical and data link layers, for example:

— X.25;

— 802.4 token bus (both broadband and carrier band);

— 802.3 CSMA/CD;

— 802.5 token ring.

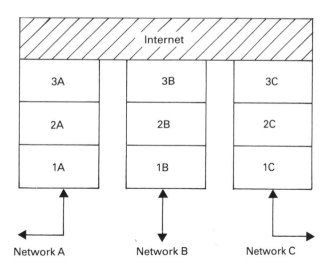

Figure 2.3   Router Architecture

THE MAP BRIDGE

The MAP bridge can be essentially thought of as providing one of
two functions: that of joining similar segments and hence exten-
ding the network beyond its original specification or that of
physically isolating segments of a single local area network from
each other. Figure 2.4 illustrates the MAP bridge architecture and
where it fits in with MAP end systems. Whichever way the MAP
bridge is used, the individual segments making up the local area
network will operate as an extended network with the following
features:

— unique addressing at the data link layer;

— a common link control protocol;

— common restrictions on packet sizes, priorities and speeds;

— the provision of message store and forward;

— the provision of broadcast/multicast capability;

— the allowed use of all IEEE 802 media access and physical
layers.

The bridge itself does not need an address because no information is meant specifically for the bridge. However, an address would
be needed for network management.

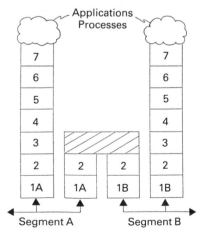

Figure 2.4   Bridge Architecture

THE MAP GATEWAY

Whether the MAP is restricted to layers 1 and 2 of the OSI model, the gateway utilises all seven layers (as depicted in Figure 2.5). The gateway is essentially a device which enables MAP networks to be connected to non-OSI and proprietary subnetworks by carrying out a protocol translation. Each of the subnetworks connected via the gateway may operate independently; the gateway can in essence be thought of as a mirror sitting between the two networks that required the connection and reflecting each of the attributes of the networks. The different attribute requirements of each of the networks connected via the gateway means that the gateway must be able to:

— store and forward messages;

— provide flow control;

— provide a virtual circuit interface;

— support network management for the various subnetworks;

— perform protocol translation.

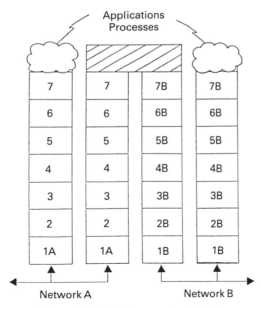

Figure 2.5 Gateway Architecture

A specification of a gateway means that it must connect networks of different types. Inevitably they will have different addressing structures, and so a gateway will have a different network address on each of the attached subnetworks (it can be thought of as a node on each of the attached networks). Gateways themselves play an important role in the architecture of communication systems because of the way the systems will have evolved over the years. They were used essentially to connect MAP networks to other networks coming from suppliers such as IBM, DEC, etc.

THE MAP/EPA SYSTEM

Typically 95% of the communications traffic within the manufactured cell will remain within that cell. The process control industry can be viewed in a similar way − in that closed loop control systems require rapid network response times in order to effectively control the processes for which they are responsible. The 5% external traffic may well represent purely the communications to the factory host computer in order to download programs containing new production schedules or to upload, from the cell, production status information. Taking this point in mind as well as the environment in which the systems are meant to operate, networks for distributed control applications require the control systems network to provide:

— fast response times for short messages;

— priority messaging schemes;

— high reliability of message transmission;

— connection to the main communications network;

— network security;

— network resiliency;

— ease of maintenance.

These requirements, essentially for the faster response times on control and time critical networks, led to the development of the enhanced performance architecture (EPA). The architecture is essentially a cut-down version of the seven-layer model using the lower 2 layers and the top layer only as illustrated in Figure 2.6. The enhanced performance architecture of MAP has been based on the work of the PROWAY Committee of the Instrument Society of America.

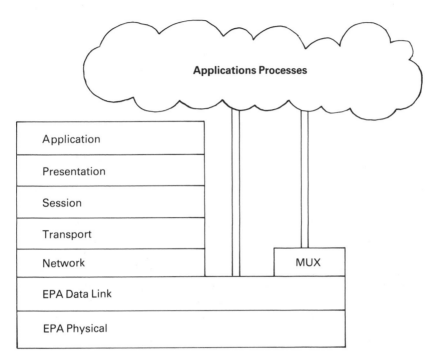

Figure 2.6   MAP/EPA Architecture

MINI MAP SYSTEM

Figure 2.6 illustrates the MAP/EPA architecture. Devices containing only the EPA side of this architecture will exist as mini MAP nodes. Full MAP nodes are OSI-compatible as they define the full seven layers of the ISO reference model architecture. However, mini MAP nodes are not OSI-compatible as they contain only the two lower layers and the top layer of the seven-layer architecture and will not be able to communicate outside of the local segment without the use of a gateway. Clearly EPA nodes are designed as the simplest nodes (for example, intelligent sensors having limited functionality)

and require only to make use of the time-critical data link services
of the architecture. A typical mini MAP node architecture is
illustrated in Figure 2.7. If any device within this architecture is
required to communicate externally to other segments it should contain the MAP/EPA dual architecture.

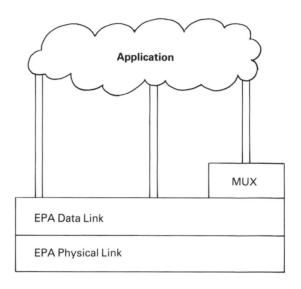

Figure 2.7   Mini-MAP Node

CONCLUSIONS

This chapter has examined the MAP architecture and the functional
building blocks which have been defined to make up that architecture and allow it to interface with other OSI and proprietary architectures. The following chapter explains the MAP specification briefly
on a layer by layer basis.

The design of any communications network is a complex business
in order to achieve the required functionality and cost-effectiveness
trade-off. This design of networks will become even more important in the future because of the requirement to take into account
not merely the diverse requirements of the business but also the
advances in technology (voice and data integration) (see Chapter 6).

3 The MAP Specification

INTRODUCTION

Chapter 1, 'Standards and Standardisation', introduced the importance of standards and the role of the International Standards Organisation's seven-layer reference model. Chapter 2 explained the MAP architecture and the way in which it was meant to fit in with existing factory layouts, both in the local environment and the more encompassing wide area environment. Chapter 3 will now explain, briefly, the MAP specification as to where it fits into the framework described in the previous two chapters.

THE PHYSICAL LAYER

There are two physical layer options available for MAP compatible nodes at the present time:

— 802.4 Broadband 10 Mbps;

— 802.4 Carrierband 5 Mbps.

The broadband specification has been part of MAP from the start. It was introduced in MAP draft version 1.0 while the carrierband specification was introduced in draft MAP version 2.2. For the future there are two additional options which are being developed:

— 802.4 Optical Fibre, using passive stars of 10 Mbps and up to 32 ports;

— 802.4 Optical Fibre with a reconfiguring dual ring configuration at 16 Mbps and up to 100 stations.

Broadband technology is part of the IEEE 802.4 (Token Bus) Communications Standard, and is recommended for backbone networks. The broadband coaxial cable specified in MAP was originally developed for CATV Applications. The cable utilises mid-split transmission (40 6-MHz channels outbound and 18 6-MHz channels inbound). The system uses a forward frequency allocation of 174 to 300 MHz (although a range of 150 to 450 MHz is possible from different manufacturers) and a reverse frequency allocation of 5 to 108 MHz.

It is possible to combine single channels into multiple adjacent channels which can then be used to carry wide band or high data rate services which would require more than the 6-MHz bandwidth. An analysis of the available frequency spectrum shows that the inbound channels above the FM bands are the channels of choice for the new frequencies. These channels are not available in mid-split systems so high-split systems will be required to take advantage of expected devices. High-split systems expand the availablity of two-way channels from 17 channels to a total of 22 or 24 channels. The high-split system uses a forward frequency allocation of 234 to 400 (+) MHz and a reverse frequency allocation of 5 to 174 MHz.

The design of the broadband network should take into consideration parameters which may affect the overall system performance. These parameters may include:

— physical considerations; for example, temperature variations in a plant, minimum bending radius of cable, positioning of the ducts for wiring;

— equipment locations; for example, positioning of amplifiers and head end equipment for ease of servicing;

— location of network test points.

The general layout of the cable is in the form of a tree configuration. This simple tree configuration can, however, be designed in a number of ways:

— simple routeing of the cable in order to cover the required plant area and provide tap coverage with the insertion of amplifiers and allowance for head ends;

— a star configuration which locates all of the amplifiers on a single site with cables fanning out to the attached devices. Although this has the advantage of all the amplifiers being protected on one site (hence giving easy maintenance and potentially higher overall reliability), the disadvantage is that the network may require more cable and amplifiers than a similar network using a non-star configuration. Increasing use of active components in a network design causes a higher probability of network failure. A trade-off should be considered;

— the distributed star configuration which is used for large sites and has clusters of amplifiers placed around the plant with each cluster connected to the head end via a trunk cable;

— in the case of very large sites or multiple plant networks, combinations of trunk cables and distributed stars may be used.

The broadband network itself is subject to path loss which is defined as RF (Radio Frequency) signal attenuation at any one frequency between the system input port and the system output port. There are inbound and outbound path losses which are defined in a broadband system. The inbound path loss is the attenuation between a distribution user outlet and a head end user port. The outbound path loss is the attenuation between a head user port and the distribution user port. The defined nominal path loss is 44 dB $+/-6$ dB inbound and 44 dB $+/-6$ dB outbound over the operating frequency range.

In situations on the plant floor where the full bandwidth of the broadband network is not required carrierband technology on coaxial cable is recommended. It comprises single-channel networks and subnetworks and is less expensive using less complex hardware. Unlike broadband which uses two different frequencies for transmission of the data (one to transmit and one to receive) thus requiring frequency translators, high-frequency filters, RF modulators and mixers; carrierband modulation is a single channel system with the whole bandwidth reserved for one network. The system does not now need to be tuned at each station, making it easier to install; and, because data is transmitted and received on the same channel, no head end is required on the network. All of this combines to make carrierband cheaper to implement and can typically be used in MAP cells.

The carrierband technology is part of the IEEE 802.4 communication standard — the data rate and modulation technique endorsed by MAP being 5 Mbps, phase coherent modulation as specified by IEEE 802.4. The carrierband segments used within a MAP network do have physical limitations due to the attenuation of the cables and taps which are used within the segment. Regenerative repeating stations between network segments remove the limit to the size or number of stations on the carrierband network. The MAP community, when implementing carrierband solutions adhere to the following guidelines:

— no more than 32 stations should be connected on single cable segment;

— the distance between the most distant stations in the logical token ring should not exceed 700m on RG-11 cable (note longer distances are possible with $\frac{1}{2}$ inch or $\frac{3}{4}$ inch solid aluminium shielded cable — this is then subject to physical limitations such as the bending radius of the cable);

— drop cable should be flexible RG-11, RG-6 or RG-59, typically not exceeding 50m in length.

Cables comprising a single channel phase coherent FSK bus medium are of a type commonly used within the CATV industry. The MAP/TOP media committee intend publishing a set of installation and media selection guidelines.

THE DATALINK LAYER

The datalink layer is divided into two sublayers:

— the media access control sub-layer (MAC);

— the logical link control sub-layer (LLC).

The IEEE 802.4 (Token Passing Bus) has been chosen as the media access control method for the MAP specification. From the physical point of view this is a token passing bus; however, logically it is a ring for the purpose of passing the actual token. One of the reasons why the token passing bus method was chosen was because it is a deterministic method: this means that the time it takes the message to get from one node to another can be exactly determined. The MAP sublayer is responsible for the handling of the token and sharing the bus with other stations and also receives data from the layers above and below the datalink layer for transmission either to the user or across the network.

The logical link control sublayer standard which is being chosen for the MAP specification is the IEEE 802.2 specification defining multipoint peer to peer protocol. Three types of service are specified in MAP version 3.0:

— connectionless oriented (type 1);

— connection oriented (type 2);

— acknowledge connection oriented (type 3).

Type 1 allows for the exchange of data between two LLCs entities without establishing a datalink connection. It does not provide message sequencing acknowledgement, flow control or error recovery.

Type 2 does establish a datalink connection and provides message sequencing acknowledgement, flow control and error recovery.

Type 3 allows for a limited frame acknowledgement, limited flow control and the retransmission on a single frame basis.

In addition to the three types of service specified there are also three classes of service which could be applied:

— Class I (supporting type 1 operation only);

— Class II (supporting types 1 and 2);

— Class III (supporting types 1 and 3).

MAP recommends Class I service or, if acknowledgements are required, Class II service. It should be noted that for increased network response (using EPA) there may be a need for the Class III response.

Probably in the use of time critical applications within a process control environment there is a need for the acknowledgement of messages to ensure that the process is properly controlled. When no higher layers exist in a MAP network (for example, mini-MAP and MAP/EPA nodes), Class III support will be required.

THE NETWORK LAYER

The network service provides for the transparent transfer of data between network service users. There are two types of OSI network service:

— connectionless-mode network service (CLNS);

— connection-mode network service (CONS).

The MAP specification supports only the connectionless-mode network service. In accordance with the internal organisations of the network layer, the network layer itself is divided into three roles:

— Sub-Network Access Protocol (SNACP);

— Sub-Network Dependent Convergence Protocol (SNDCP);

— Sub-Network Independent Convergence Protocol (SNICP).

The ISO End System to Intermediate System protocol is supported as a mandatory protocol in order to facilitate a dynamic routeing scheme. This allows end systems (ES) to obtain addresses of intermediate systems (IS) reachable in one hop. It also allows intermediate systems to obtain the addresses of all the ES on its subnetwork. There is not a suitable protocol available for IS to IS routeing, therefore IS systems must keep tables of other reachable IS systems.

To achieve connection oriented to connectionless oriented subnetworks a router utilising an SNDCP is used. This area is the subject of ongoing work as connection oriented to connectionless interworking is a recognised priority.

THE TRANSPORT LAYER

The transport layer defined by MAP is given as Class IV of the ISO compatible subset of the National Bureau of Standards. Class IV, the richest of the transport classes, is used in order to compensate for the functions loss by using a connectionless service or the link layer. As well as connection, data transfer and disconnection as provided by Class 0, the simplest class, Class IV, provides multiplexing of transport connections, flow control, checking for out-of-sequence data, an expedited data service, error detection and re-synchronisation after errors (see Chapter 1). As a consequence of using a Connection Oriented Network Service (CONS) over X.25, some consideration is being given to the inclusion of Class 0 protocol.

THE SESSION LAYER

MAP specifies the ISO Session Standard using full duplex communication. A subset of the basic combined subset (BCS) is all that is required to support the higher layer services in 3.0 versions of the specification. The scope of the applications is increasing, and consequently additional session layer functions are being introduced. The basic activity subset (BAS) provides all BCS capabilities plus exception reporting, some synchronisation and activity management. The session layer services available to the presentation layer are defined in terms of functional units. The functional units are logical groupings of related services and are negotiated by the peer session service users during connection establishment phase. The stages of the session layer itself comprise:

— session connection establishment;

— data transfer;

— session connection release.

For MAP connectivity the minimum subset of the ISO session layer International Standard is required – the kernel functional unit and the duplex functional unit.

THE PRESENTATION LAYER

It is the task of the presentation layer to carry out the negotiation of transfer syntaxes and to provide for the transformation to and from these transfer syntaxes. One of the major steps in the evolution of the MAP specification has been the inclusion of the kernel

presentation services into the MAP version 3.0 specification at draft
international level, together with the use of abstract syntax nota-
tion 1 (ASN.1) encoding in certain application service and protocol
standards. The ASN.1 language is used to define the type and values
of a data item and the collections of data items without specifying
the exact bits representation of information. The presentation kernel
services allow for the establishment of a connection which will use
a selected encoding of a selected abstract syntax. The MAP 3.0
specification covers the protocol agreements and is devoted to the
issues involved with the negotiation of transfer syntaxes and the
responsibilities of the presentation protocol. The following functional unit is required for all systems:

— presentation kernel functional unit which supports the basic
  presentation services required to establish a presentation connection, transfer normal data and release the presentation
  connection. It should be noted that this is a non-negotiable
  functional unit.

THE APPLICATION LAYER

As described in Chapter 1, the application layer provides services
to the end users' applications and does not contain the application
programmes. The application layer of the MAP specification contains specifics such as ACSE, Directory Services, CASE, FTAM,
MMS and virtual terminal.

ACSE is included in MAP version 3.0 and provides for connection establishment and connection release to manage interapplica-
tion communication. It is intended to provide a standard service
for applications to communicate common parameters such as titles,
addresses and application context during the request for an association. It is the common application service element (CASE) which
includes the set of association control service elements (ACSE).
CASE provides common facilities required by specific application
service elements (SASE). A much quoted example of specific
application service elements is the elements required in an airline
booking system.

The Directory Services specified in MAP 3.0 solve the directory
needs of the single enterprise domain. A future work item of the

MAP Committee is to address the multiple-enterprise domain problem. The MAP directory system allows user friendly references to
network objects. This allows references which are made to the network to be much more stable. Additions, deletions and any changes
in the physical location of network objects thus remain invisible
to users who use the directory services. The directory system comprises the following elements:

— Directory Information Base (DIB);

— Directory Service Agent (DSA);

— Directory User Agent (DUA);

— User.

A client issues an update or query to its DUA, which forwards
the request to a DSA using the directory access protocol (DAP).
The collection of information is made by the directory system in
the DIB. In order to satisfy the requirements for the distribution
and management of a DIB and to ensure that objects can be unam-
biguously named and their entries found, a flat structure of entries
is not possible and so a hierarchial structure is used with the DIB
being accessed through the DSA.

The file transfer, access and management (FTAM) specification
provides a set of services for conveniently transferring information
between application processors and file stores. It guarantees the
ability to:

— work with binary or text files;

— create files;

— delete files;

— transfer entire files;

— read file attributes;

— change file attributes;

— erase file contents;

— locate specific records;

— read and write records of a file.

In addition the following file types may be optionally supported:

— sequential files;

— random access files;

— single key indexed sequential files.

The FTAM standard defines a virtual file store which is used for describing the service provided by the FTAM service element. The FTAM file store is used to map FTAM services to the local file store.

The manufacturing message service (MMS) is a communications protocol standard for manufacturing applications. Although MMS is applicable to a wide range of plant applications the standard does not contain information on specific applications. MMS can be thought of as providing a kernel standard in that it specifies how messages are assembled and sent but does not contain application-specific information. The application-specific information, necessary for interoperability of plant floor equipment, is intended to be supplied by companion standards to MMS.

It had been recognised that a virtual terminal service allowing device-independent transactions and thus enabling any terminal to access any computer system on the network would be a useful addition. Work is still progressing in this area.

SUMMARY

This chapter has given a very brief overview to the MAP specification. The reader's attention is drawn to the standards used in the MAP specification, listed in Appendix 2. Further information on the MAP specification itself should be obtained via the local chapter of the MAP User Group. Attention is also drawn to a more detailed publication by the National Computing Centre on MAP 2.1 and MAP 3.0. The MAP specification is still evolving, in a controlled way.

Further work areas under consideration are network management and security. Progress of this work is dependent upon the rate of development of the base standards themselves.

The specification itself is complex because the base standards which are used within the specification are complex. It is because of this inherent complexity that testing is in itself a complex business. The next chapter explains some of the requirements for testing.

4   Testing MAP Implementations

INTRODUCTION

This chapter introduces the concepts of testing which are not uniquely the domain of MAP. The concepts which will be described apply to any system which is based on an open systems interconnection architecture. In addition to the requirements of testing an OSI based system, the various testing relationships are also explained and an introduction into the organisations involved in the testing is given.

WHY TEST MAP IMPLEMENTATIONS?

Without some form of structured testing, the concept behind MAP – and therefore MAP itself – could not and would not exist. There must be a mechanism in place whereby the common rules being implemented within different pieces of equipment can be assessed.

MAP is already becoming of major strategic importance to organisations, both in forward planning for new equipment and in deciding where within the company to implement the MAP network (see Chapter 6). Because of this strategic importance to organisations it would be very dangerous not to go through a program of rigorous and controlled testing before equipment is 'let loose' on the factory floor. The standards which have been used to define each of the individual layers of MAP are inherently complex in order to allow for the necessary functionality of each layer and to provide the required interworking during both normal and error conditions. This inherent complexity impacts on the interpretation and implementation of the standards at each layer and inevitably leaves the door open for suppliers to implement the MAP specification in different ways. Testing MAP implementations is not just limited to suppliers' requirements. It may be required for other reasons, such as:

— supplier development testing of the product;

— supplier quality assurance testing prior to the release of the product;

— acceptance testing of the products by the end user community.

It is inevitable − if questions regarding implementation issues within a suppliers' product are left open − that, during any interworking phase between suppliers, emotions will run high regarding who has provided the correct interpretation of the specification within the product. Testing must be carried out so that both parties − user and supplier − are satisfied at their outcome and have confidence in the results.

THIRD-PARTY TESTING

The underlying aim of MAP is to allow different products from a number of different suppliers to be successfully interworked within a multivendor environment. The MAP specification is based on a complex set of communications protocols, the testing of which is a relatively new activity and for this reason the test results will need to be interpreted by an expert familiar with the relevant protocol. Users may view the results as lacking in objectivity if the vendors themselves carry out the testing of their MAP implementations. Third-party testing stems from the recognition of the need for objectivity and independence in executing the tests, interpreting the results, and maintaining the test systems.

Third-party testing of MAP products will give users of those products the confidence required that they conform to the MAP specification. The MAP product certification process will be of use only when stated by an independent third-party tester and will always remain of dubious value if claims of conformance are made purely by the supplier without a tester's endorsement.

Testing of MAP implementations does not stop at conformance testing, it is only the first step in the process.

THE TESTING REQUIREMENTS

The testing requirements can be split into five categories:

— conformance testing;

— interoperability testing;

— acceptance testing;

— applications testing;

— performance testing.

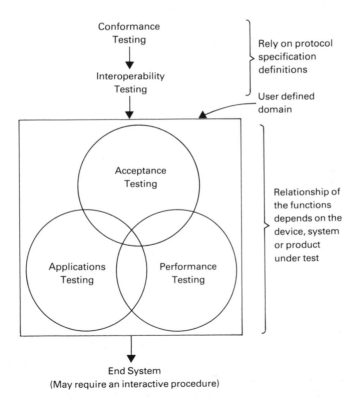

Figure 4.1   Testing Interrelationships

Compliance testing is another area which, in the future, will receive more attention. It essentially encompasses a description of the testing of protocol stacks (introduced in Chapter 1) with respect to MAP, TOP, GOSIP, etc. The details of compliance testing are not looked at in this book. However, some of the testing requirements described above are included.

All the testing requirements demand different approaches. The relationship of the various areas with respect to product testing environments is shown in Figure 4.1.

CONFORMANCE TESTING

Conformance testing itself is application independent. Taking a robot through all of its movements or a milling machine through a preprogrammed cutting sequence does not constitute conformance testing, even though the equipment may have MAP interfaces installed. Testing of the sequences are required but conformance testing actually means testing the method by which the application software will eventually reach its intended target machine.

Due to the inherent complexity of the communications protocols which make up the MAP specification, one hundred per cent testing of the implementation is impractical due to the vast number of possible combinations of conditions which could occur during a communications session. The only way to proceed is to take a representative sample of states and sequences and to apply these to the implementation under test. Clearly the communications sequences (test cases) which are to be applied and used for the tests must be agreed by all third-party testers involved; otherwise the outcome would be the generation of different test results depending upon which third-party tester actually tested the implementation. Conformance testing will only be as good as the specification it is meant to test. The more thoroughly the specification is verified, the more effective conformance testing will become.

The evolution of MAP has seen minor and major revisions of the specification. Major revisions of the specification are depicted by the transition from version 1 to version 2 to version 3. Minor revisions of the MAP specification have been seen through the transition from, for example, version 2.1 to 2.2. The critical factor behind revision transitions is that major revision transitions result in incompatibilities between products implemented to different versions. This means that products which are following the major revisions of the MAP specifications will require formal conformance testing at each major revision. Minor revisions of the specifications may not require formal conformance testing because the specification has been defined so that these minor revisions remain interoperable.

MAP conformance testing will require the following facilities (considered below):

— a conformance test system;

— a conformance test suite;

— conformance testing procedures.

Conformance Test System

The philosophy of conformance testing is illustrated in Figure 4.2. The upper and lower testers in each of the systems described act as controllers and observers of the activity at the layer boundaries of the implementation under test (IUT). The difference between the upper and lower testers in each of the systems is the level of control and observation available to them at each of the boundaries.

The first system offers the most control and observation because the upper and lower testers reside directly on the implementation of the test. This is a typical situation occurring during product development by an implementor. The drawback with this system is that it is impossible to test an implementation in its normal environment, ie communicating real data using the layer below.

The second system in Figure 4.2 offers no control or observation at the upper boundary and only limited and indirect control at the lower boundary. The limited access afforded by this system restricts the depth to which conformance testing can be carried out. It does however have a benefit in that the system can be applied in general to any implementation. Control of the upper boundary can be achieved in a very indirect way if some application is running above the implementation of the test. By driving the implemen-

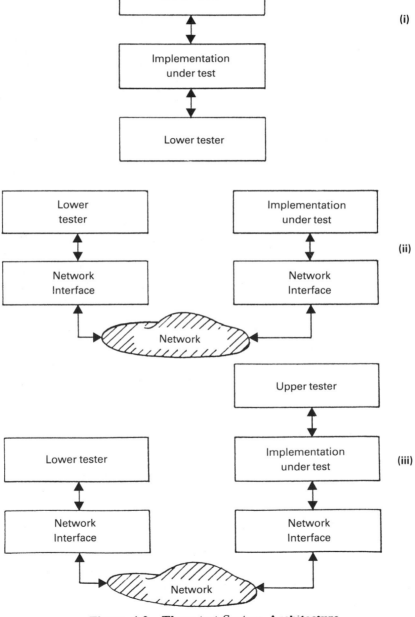

Figure 4.2   Three-test System Architecture

tation of the test at the lower boundary, the application then gives a marginal degree of control and observation.

The third system combines the second system with an upper tester or 'predictable user' which resides above the implementation under test. This system may be applied when the upper boundary (service interface) is available and control and observation can be supplied by the upper tester. This system is preferred if access is available at the upper boundary. However, it does require a predictable user to be able to interface with the implementation under test.

As described in Chapter 3, the MAP specification comprises a stack of communications protocols. A critical issue in conformance testing is the use of single or multilayer testing. In order to test a single layer access is required at both boundaries of the layer implementation. This service access is not a mandatory requirement and consequently enables implementors a degree of freedom when designing implementations for specific requirements. When a situation arises where a service interface cannot be accessed, conformance testing must be carried out by multilayer testing. Multilayer testing presents its own inherent problems in that in order to exercise a specific layer it may be necessary to go through one or more layers. This may restrict the ability to be able to functionally exercise the layer in question. It is a direct requirement of conformance testing that it must be necessary to edit outgoing protocol data units and create spontaneous errors with respect to the implementation under test. The implementation will thus be tested for what it cannot do as well as what it was designed to do.

Conformance Test Suite

Conformance test suites consist of specific test cases, each one covering a different area of the protocol. The combination of these test cases which form the test suite are designed to give an adequate depth of coverage to the testing and so provide a reasonable guarantee of interworking. A typical test system architecture is shown in Figure 4.3 and comprises pairs of complementary test scenarios. One scenario will drive the test centres reference implementation while the other drives the implementation under test. These are then used to define the service behaviour of the communicating entities.

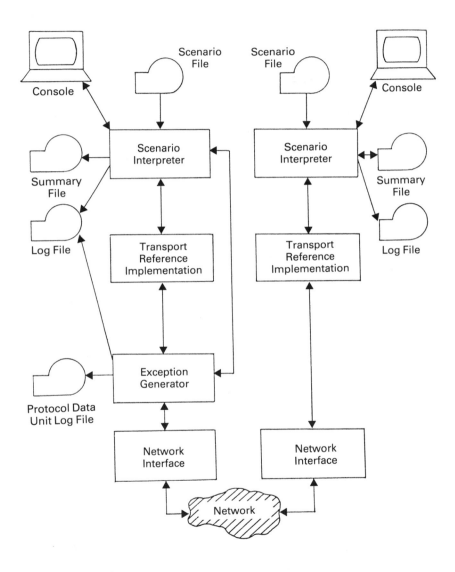

Figure 4.3   NCC Transport Test System Architecture

Conformance Testing Procedures

Conformance testing is split into two parts: *static testing* and *dynamic testing*.

Static conformance testing is the first step in the conformance testing procedures and requires the assessment of claims made by the supplier of MAP products to be looked at with respect to the requirements demanded by the MAP specification. The claims themselves are made in a protocol implementation conformance statement (PICS). Within this initial review any optional areas of the specification which have been included in the product by the supplier are also identified. If the assessor from a third-party testing organisation is satsified that the static conformance test proves that the implementation does conform then the product may proceed on to the next stage − dynamic testing.

The dynamic conformance testing stage will take place only after static conformance testing has been successfully negotiated. This stage will make use of the test systems and test suites available in order to exercise the implementation and establish its conformance with the relevant specifications and standards. It is during this stage that any options which the supplier claims to have implemented will be evaluated.

Conformance testing will not supply an automatic result of a pass/fail nature. MAP conformance testing is no different in this respect; it still requires human interpretation of the results.

Conformance testing covers all of the procedures and associated documentation with respect to:

— following an initial contract between the implementor and third-party testing organisation;

— static conformance testing;

— dynamic conformance testing;

— the production and delivery of a test report to the supplier.

A product's conformance to the MAP specification, both static and dynamic, does not guarantee interworking. There is a requirement for interoperability testing.

Interoperability Testing

Ensuring devices can communicate with each other is only achievable through interoperability testing. Interworking between devices is not necessarily a transative relationship. Hence, if system A can communicate with system B and system B can communicate with system C it does not necessarily follow that system A can communicate with system C. Unlike conformance testing this means that interoperability is, to some extent, applications dependent. Testing for interoperability can take two forms, *passive testing* or *active testing*.

Passive interoperability testing simply monitors the communication between the two communicating implementations. This form of testing does not interfere with the communications between the two implementations and will not force the implementations into handling errors by injecting errors itself.

Active interoperability testing uses a test system to actually inject errors and so test the implementation's error handling capabilities. With any test system repeatability of the test is essential and if this is achievable with active interoperability testing it is clear that this is the system which is more beneficial to end users.

Acceptance Testing

Acceptance testing defines the joint testing period between the end user and the supplier before equipment is effectively 'signed off'. It is clear that the acceptance testing procedure should require some evidence of formal conformance testing and interoperability. Acceptance testing must combine the disciplines of MAP conformance testing and interoperability with the specification laid down by the supplier for the operation of his equipment and relate these to the functional requirements which the equipment is meant to satisfy in the user's environment.

Applications Testing

At this stage MAP conformance testing should remain in the background. However, as was stated previously, interoperability testing is to some extent applications dependent and it may be necessary to take the interoperability results into account. Although interoperability should be taken into account in applications testing it should not constitute the main part of the testing. Organisations who are used to carrying out applications testing for equipment within their company at the present time should view the area of applications testing within MAP in exactly the same way. The applications which are being evaluated should be oblivious to the communications methods (MAP or otherwise) which will be used.

Performance Testing

Suppliers of products to satisfy certain market requirements rely on their own equipment out-performing other suppliers' equipment. There are essentially two aspects concerned with performance testing:

— measurement of the efficiency of the protocol itself;

— measurement of the efficiency of the implementation of the protocol within the suppliers' equipment.

The performance testing of MAP systems is application dependent in addition to being dependent on the processing efficiency of the particular implementation. This processing efficiency will typically depend on the load, memory requirements, response time requirements and buffer management defined within the system designed.

SUPPORT FOR MAP CONFORMANCE TESTING

A number of organisations have supported MAP conformance testing by developing in some cases, and using in others, test systems based on MAP version 2.1. Among these organisations are the Industrial Technology Institute in the USA, the Fraunhoffer Institute in Germany whose interest in the MAP test services stems from its involvement in a European ESPRIT project (Communications Networks for Manufacturing Applications) and its requirements to support this project with testing, and finally the Networking Centre in the UK which was awarded a contract by the Department of Trade and Industry to provide MAP 2.1 test services to UK industry. These organisations have suffered because the market has not been there essentially for MAP 2.1 testing which essentially proceeded on an ad hoc basis.

Future developments in MAP test systems are much more interesting and should help to stabilise the whole area. The key factors in this future development are:

— the freezing of MAP version 3.0;

— the involvement of the Corporation for Open Systems in the USA;

— the Enterprise Network Event to be held in the USA and to demonstrate MAP (and TOP) version 3.

The core of the testing of MAP version 3 will be based upon the test services developed by the Corporation for Open Systems. Much of this so called 'COS platform' will be based upon test suites developed by the National Computing Centre in the UK under contract to COS.

The second factor is the Corporation for Open Systems itself because as a member organisation which can boast the support of the world's major computer manufacturers it is inevitable that market forces will demand that a substantial proportion of the networking products on offer will conform to the COS platform. The Corporation for Open Systems has, as part of its charter, defined its intention to provide conformance test services to its membership and to other computer product members.

The third factor is the Enterprise Network Event in the USA which demonstrates the availability of MAP 3.0 products and will require conformance test services for these products. COS test services will not cover all of the protocols required by MAP version 3 and in this respect European organisations will be providing some subcontractual support in addition to the major provision of test suites to COS by the National Computing Centre. The organisations and test systems to be supplied will be:

— the Fraunhoffer Institute will provide manufacturing message service, 7 and 2 layer, network management, 7 and 2 layer and directory services, 7 and 2 layer;

— the Networking Centre will provide logical link control 3, end system to intermediate system routeing protocol and routers;

— Leeds University will provide IGES V3 test capability.

Clearly the rationalisation of test suite availability between different organisations in different countries is happening. Even though the test suites will then become available there are still the key issues of identification and accreditation of the individual test centres within each country and the rules concerning the certification of the MAP products. It is clear that the first step towards international certification of MAP conforming products is the identification of accredited test centres.

5 Support for MAP

Support for MAP can effectively be broken down into three areas:

— user support;

— supplier support;

— other organisations (eg academic institutions, test houses).

MAP, although being instigated by General Motors in the United States of America, has benefited through a number of demonstration projects concerned with MAP. The demonstration projects have tended to concentrate the mind on the development of the MAP specification and have laid down milestones and goals. An early demonstration of MAP took place at the National Computer Conference in Las Vegas in 1984. The following year the Autofact Exhibition took place and resulted in a demonstration of MAP version 2.1. This demonstration also resulted in the provision of test tools for MAP version 2.1 in order to test Internet, transport layer, session layer, CASE, FTAM and MMFS. The Industrial Technology Institute in Michigan was then given the Autofact test tools and started on a programme to extend and improve them.

Demonstrations of MAP have not been limited to the American Continent. In November 1986 the UK Department of Trade and Industry initiated the CIMAP event which was inspired by Autofact but concentrated on MAP version 2.1 implementation with errata.

Europe has not been slow in initiating programmes concerning manufacturing communications and during the time which the MAP initiative was taking place an ESPRIT programme was underway. The programme of interest within ESPRIT concerns project number 955, called Communications Networks for Manufacturing Applications (CNMA). This project built on the development which had already taken place on MAP 2.1 but considerably extended it with respect to manufacturing message systems and took into account the requirements for European companies regarding the communications architecture.The ESPRIT programme is continuing and will build considerably upon the OSI expertise in Europe.

Support for the MAP initiative shows no sign of slowing down. However, with any development of this sort there will be consolidation periods whereby the development of the specification will stop allowing the suppliers of equipment to catch up and allow them to do what they are actually in business for − building and selling products to supply the marketplace. The consolidation period stops MAP becoming a moving target as far as product development is concerned.

MAP has been a user defined initiative, not merely through General Motors, but with many other large organisations within the USA and throughout the world. There are now MAP user groups in the Far East as well as the American continent and Europe, and even a World Federation. It is recognised that MAP can only succeed if products built in one part of the world and which have undergone recognised testing procedures are totally acceptable in another part of the world without having to go through a similar testing routine. Although MAP is a user instigated programme, without supplier support, it is not feasible. The suppliers themselves obviously have their own inherent interests at heart but the willingness to work together with other suppliers has already been shown.

The MAP specification will steadily change in the future. This change will come through the support and influence of the needs of other organisations; for example, the process control industry.

Appendix 3 gives a list of some of the organisations who are involved with the development of the MAP specification and the related services required to support that specification and to make implementation possible.

6 The Future

Chapter 5 described the support that MAP has received from various organisations; Chapter 4 introduced the problems of migration and compatibility. These issues are critical because as MAP takes its place in the communications hierarchies of organisations the support it receives is the difference between success and failure. By the same token it will only receive support to the extent to which it provides what the user wants. This chapter is meant to put MAP into perspective and help organisations come to terms with the positioning of MAP within their own company. MAP was a means to an end for General Motors. However, the functions which MAP provides, and the solution it is putting forward to communications problems, must be kept in perspective with an organisation's overall communications and business requirements.

Organisations going through the process of evaluating MAP for use within their own company should understand that MAP will not satisfy everyone's requirements immediately. The qualification of this statement arises primarily from the fact that not all of the industrial communications networks evolve at the same rate. If a sample is taken from the sufficiently large population of industrial companies then it can be found through an analysis of their communications networks that the results will tend towards a Gaussian (or normal) distribution (see Figure 6.1).

This suggests that there will always be companies on the extreme right of the side of this distribution − the type of company already heavily committed to installing networking and automation equipment in its plants. By the same reasoning there will always be companies on the extreme left hand side of the distribution − those companies only just beginning to think about networking.

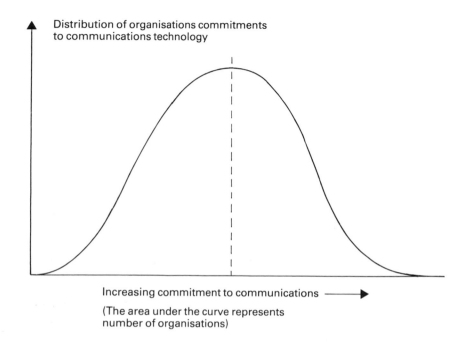

Figure 6.1   Distribution of Companies Committed to
Communications

The majority of companies fall somewhere within the middle ground. They may already have some communications in place (not necessarily networks) but almost certainly each constituent part of the communications facility will have evolved in its own unique way. This is true not only of manufacturing data but also of voice communication and non-manufacturing data. (Non-manufacturing data cannot logically exist in a manufacturing organisation whose prime function is the production of saleable units. However, for the sake of clarity, I will continue to refer to manufacturing data as, for example, part programs; and non-manufacturing data as, for example, financial information.)

The remainder of this chapter gives pointers on how to evaluate whether MAP is applicable for particular communications requirements.

The consistent analysis of the distribution described above is made more complex when geographical regional variations are taken into account (the needs and expertise of organisations within Europe do not follow exactly the same pattern of similar organisations in the United States – where MAP originated). Thus we may conclude that the evolution of an organisation's network and the definition of its future networking requirements depend ultimately on:

— the positioning of the organisation in relation to the normal distribution described above;

— the future networking needs of the organisation in relation to its corporate plan;

— the ability of technology to satisfy those needs in a cost-effective way;

— the availability of the technology within the organisation's geographical area.

Keeping these four points in mind, we can now use General Motors as an example and examine its present and future requirements and where MAP would fit in. Applying the previous normal distribution model to the General Motors environment we find, through an analysis of the four points, that:

— General Motors are a company predominantly on the right hand side of this distribution curve and as such their capital expenditure on new plant automation equipment was, and is, colossal. They needed to buy equipment from many different vendors in order to satisfy specific plant needs and consequently there was a requirement for the equipment to interwork, not just to interface. This immediately caused problems because of the proprietary communications used by each particular vendor. General Motors were spending increasing amounts of money on 'black boxes' to allow different types of equipment to talk to each other.

— In relation to the corporate plan, General Motors saw itself spending more in the future on automation equipment and consequently, because of its present situation, more on the 'black boxes' which had become essential for effective communications. The need had arisen for a common communications protocol serving all equipment.

— The current technology was able to provide a solution but not in a cost effective way due to the increased spending on 'black boxes'.

— General Motors already had in place a number of communications networks — a basic infrastructure — but what was needed was the definition of a protocol stack encompassing the users' requirements. In addition there were international standards available for use but there were also recognised holes.

We have seen that the outcome of this analysis led to the definition of the MAP architecture as described in Chapter 2 and the MAP specification described in Chapter 3. It is only when MAP is then used within the corporate network architecture that problems start to arise, at the present time due to a number of fundamental reasons:

— MAP is still an evolving specification and as such presents the user community with a somewhat moving target, although General Motors has gone some way towards solving this problem by attempting to freeze the MAP version 3.0 specification for a number of years.

— Broadband installations are more common in the USA than in Europe, although again there is increased support for MAP protocols over Ethernet.

— Many organisations already have their networks based on Ethernet, baseband systems.

So where does this leave MAP networks which are based purely on broadband? Clearly unless organisations are fortunate enough to have the benefit of a 'green field' site the main requirement is for a migration strategy incorporating broadband or carrierband (organisations in the USA do not have to justify the underlying broadband network first — it is usually already in place!). In order to find the level where MAP will fit into a corporate network (see Chapter 2, Figure 2.2), the following guidelines are recommended:

— plan and install broadband (this is a non-trivial task and should not be underestimated). Analysis of requirements may show that carrierband is more appropriate;

— define the voice and data requirements (MAP specifies PBX connections);

— define the information flows within the plant;

— define the eventual communications architecture within the plant;

— define the wide area network communications requirements.

If these guidelines are followed it will be easier to establish which equipment will be affected by MAP and to take account of this in invitations to tender for future needs.

It must be concluded that there can be no hard and fast rule for the adoption of MAP within any organisation. Given N different companies there are likely to be N different migration plans. This is not meant as a 'get out' but must be accepted as a fact of life. The 'bottom line' questions to be asked in relation to the direction of communications technology are:

What will MAP give me?

Are the products available?

Will it be cost effective to implement?

These are not straightforward questions and must be viewed with the company's long-term strategy in mind. Trying to answer these questions based on an organisation's short-term requirements is foolhardy.

Taken in relation to an organisation's corporate strategy and the suppliers' attitude to MAP — as the use of proprietary networks can still form part of the migration path towards MAP — answering the questions above should point the way to where MAP can be placed within an organisation's corporate communications hierarchy.

If organisations look at the prospect of using MAP it will force them at least to scrutinise their own, often neglected, corporate communications infrastructure. In consequence they will be better placed to assess their own future requirements with respect to the more fundamental issue — that of integration.

Appendix 1

Glossary

ABM

Asynchronous Balanced Mode; a mode of operation defined within HDLC which covers point-to-point communication. Polling is not required and either station is allowed to transmit without permission from the other. This is identical to LAPB. There are a number of other modes of operation within HDLC.

Abstract Transfer Syntax

Part of the presentation layer but specified by entities in the application layer, it is concerned with the type of information to be transferred. Together with a compatible CTS is referred to as presentation context.

Acknowledge

Message sent by receiving station to indicate that a frame has been received without errors.

ACSE

Associated Control Service Elements. Functions defined as part of the application layer, common to a number of application services (DIS 8649/2 and DIS 8650/20).

ADCCP

Advanced Data Communications Control Protocol; a bit-oriented synchronised data link control protocol standard adopted by ANSI. Functionally identical to HDLC.

ADD   Addendum to OSI full international standard (eg ISO 8348/ADD1).

Addressing   This is a critical issue particularly at the network layer where ISO 8348/ADD2 exists. Work is required at a national level to decide upon an actual numbering scheme in line with ISO goals.

Alternate Routeing   A technique used within networks for varying the route of the traffic depending upon loading and availability of channels. Particularly used in packet switched networks.

ANSA   Advanced Network Systems Architecture; a UK Alvey project to investigate performance effect OSI.

ANSI   American National Standards Institute; US standards organisation.

Application-entity   The part of an application process which concerns OSI.

Application Process   An OSI term to describe a user of the OSI infrastructure — whether it be an application program, a human operator or a process control device.

Architecture   A framework for a computer or communications system which defines its functions, interfaces and procedures.

ASCII   The American Standard Code for Information Interchange; based on the ISO 7-bit data code, usually transmitted in 8-bit data code incorporated a parity bit.

ASN.1	Abstract Syntax Notation One; part of the OSI presentation layer standards (ISO 8824 and ISO 8825).
Asynchronous	Simple communication of data character by character which generally relies on a host for screen formatting.
AUTOFACT	US trade show at which MAP and TOP demonstrations have taken place.
BAS	Basic Activity Subset; one of the defined subsets of the session layer (ISO 8326 and ISO 8327).
BCS	Basic Combined Subset; one of the defined subsets of the session layer.
Bit	Binary digit; when referred to in bits per second (or bps) it indicates the transmission rate of a communications link.
Blocking	A function which takes multiple SDUs from the layer above and creates a single PDU.
Bridge	A device that allows two similar LANs using the same protocol to be interconnected. No modification is made to either the content or format of the data passing through the device.
Broadband	A LAN signalling technique that utilises frequency division multiplexing (FDM) to carry many independent channels simultaneously. Generally uses either a one or two cable system as its physical transmission medium.

BSI   British Standards Institution.

BSS   Basic Synchronised Subset; one of the
                                     defined subsets of the session layer
                                     (ISO 8326 and OSI 8327).

CASE   Common Application Service
                                     Elements; a set of OSI layer 7 stan-
                                     dards which provide common func-
                                     tions for the application programs and
                                     other application layer standards (DIS
                                     8649 and DIS 8650). No longer widely
                                     used – more likely to see ACSE and
                                     CCR.

CCITT   The International Consultative Com-
                                     mittee on Telephony and Telegraphy
                                     (part of the International Telecom-
                                     munication Union, an agency of the
                                     UN); one of the leading international
                                     standards-making organisations, com-
                                     prising mainly PTTs (national postal,
                                     telephone and telegraphy organ-
                                     isations).

CCR   Commitment, Concurrency and
                                     Recovery; functions defined as part of
                                     CASE which are common to many
                                     specific applications (DIS 8649/3 and
                                     DIS 8650/3).

CEN   European Committee for Standardisa-
                                     tion. European counter part of ISO.

CENELEC   European Committee for Elec-
                                     trotechnical Standardisation. Euro-
                                     pean counterpart of IEC.

CEPT   European Conference of Posts and
                                     Telecommunications. CCITT counter-
                                     part for Europe.

CIM   Computer Integrated Manufacture; manufacture controlled and co-ordinated by computers with only minimal human intervention.

Circuit-switching   One of the major classes of network, whereby a circuit is established and maintained between the communicating parties for the duration of the 'call' (on the public telephone network) and is then disconnected, in contrast with 'non-switched' communications over point-to-point links.

Class Negotiation   Used in the transport protocol, a process whereby specific options are selected for a particular connection.

CLNS   Connectionless Network Service.

Concrete Transfer Syntax (CTS)   Used to represent information transferred between end systems as agreed between those end systems. It is part of the presentation layer.

Connectionless Service Where no permanent connection can be assumed, and no connection establishment takes place prior to communication.

Connection-oriented   Where a permanent connection (either logical or physical) exists for the duration of the communication.

CONS   Connection-Oriented Network Service.

COS   Corporation for Open Systems; US-based organisation sponsored by a number of suppliers and large users, involved in research, standards development and standards promotion.

COTP   Connection-Oriented Transport Protocol.

CSMA/CD   Carrier Sense Multiple Access/Collision Detection; one of the major classes of low-level network technology, and a method of preventing data corruption used mainly for local area networks (LANs). Ethernet is an example of this type. It is specified in OSI Standard ISO 8802/3, based upon the work of IEEE committee 802.3.

Cyclic Redundancy Check (CRC)   Scheme for error detection employed by HDLC.

DAD   Addendum to a standard at DIS status (eg ISO 8073/DAD2).

Data Link Control   The second layer of the OSI reference model at which blocks of data are reliably transmitted over an imperfect transmission link.

DCE   Data Circuit Termination Equipment; a CCITT term referring to equipment which carries out signal conversion and coding on the line (eg a modem or equivalent).

DIS   Draft International Standard; final stage prior to becoming a full international standard from ISO (eg DIS 7942).

DP
Draft Proposal; a proposed standard from ISO at the first stage of development but with some technical stability (eg DP 8613).

DTE
Data Terminal Equipment; a CCITT term referring to the terminal or computer equipment which is the origin or destination of data traffic. A DCE is required for connection to remote DTE.

ECMA
European Computer Manufacturers Association (a trade organisation very active in international standards-making).

EIA
Electronic Industries Association (a US based standards organisation, principally concerned with low-level electrical interfaces).

EN
European Norme; a standard within the European Community.

End system
Strictly used in the OSI context to define an 'open system' that can communicate with other end systems via OSI protocols, as distinct from a Relay or Gateway that performs an intermediate routeing function.

Entity
Active element within one OSI layer which employs the services of the next lower layer to communicate with a peer entity.

ENV
European pre-standards from CEN/CENELEC/CEPT.

ESPRIT   European Strategic Programme of
                               Research in Information Technology.

Ethernet   A type of local area network based
                               upon CSMA/CD technology —
                               originally developed by DEC, Intel
                               and Xerox.

EurOSInet   European demonstration of an OSI
                               network by a number of leading
                               vendors.

Frame   A unit of HDLC. A sequence of bits
                               which make up a valid message, con-
                               taining flags, control field, address
                               field, a frame check sequence, and
                               optionally an information field.

FTAM   File Transfer, Access and Manage-
                               ment — of the protocols being
                               developed for the OSI application
                               layer; specified in DIS 8571.

Functional Standards   Identified 'stacks' of base standards
                               to allow the construction of inter-
                               working products.

Gateway   An intermediate system in the com-
                               munication between two or more *end
                               systems* which are not directly linked
                               and/or observe different *protocols* (eg
                               between an OSI systems and a non-
                               OSI system).

GKS   Graphics Kernel System; standards for
                               computer graphics, current reference
                               is ISO 7942.

GOSIP   Government OSI Profile — in the UK
                               and USA.

HDLC   High-level Data Link Control; a standard for frame structures in connection with data communications protocols, at the data link layer (ISO 3309 is concerned with HDLC frame structure).

Host   A computer system on which applications can be executed and which also provides a service to connected users and devices.

IEC   International Electrotechnical Commission.

IEEE   Institute of Electrical and Electronic Engineers (of America); another organisation active in standards-making, mainly relevant for LANs.

Interconnection   A term often used to define a lesser level than full *interworking,* such that two computer systems can communicate and exchange data but without consideration of how the dialogue between *applications processes* is controlled or how the data is presented and recognised.

Interworking   Ultimately, the achievement of proper and effective communication of 'linking' between different *applications processes* or programs and data, may be on different systems from different manufacturers, remote from each other and connected by some transmission medium or network.

IS   International Standard; fully agreed and published ISO standard (eg ISO 7498).

ISDN   Integrated Services Digital Network; this will be OSI-compatible at the lower layers.

ISO   International Standards Organisation; major body responsible for the development of OSI standards.

IT   Information Technology; a term used to encompass the methods and techniques used in information handling and retrieval by automatic means, including computing, telecommunications and office systems.

JTM   Job Transfer and Manipulation; one of the protocols being developed for the OSI application layer for activating and controlling remote processing (DP 8831 and 8832).

Kernel   Service elements within the session layer which are necessary to set up and close down a connection; part of ISO 8326 and ISO 8327. Also used to describe basic elements of CASE (DIS 8649 and DIS 8650).

LAN   Local Area Network; spans a limited geographical area (usually a building or a site) and interconnects a variety of computers and other devices, usually at very high data rates.

LAPB   Link Access Procedure Balanced; a variant of HDLC used between peer systems, which is the basis for layer 2 of X.25 (as an example of standards in this area. ISO 7776 is concerned with X.25 LAPB compatible DTE Data Link Procedure).

Layer

In the OSI Reference Mode, used to define a discrete level of function within a communications context with a defined *service* interface — alternative *protocols* for a particular layer should then be interchangeable without impact on adjoining layers.

LLC1 AND LLC2

Logical Link Control One and Two; level 2 protocols defined for LANs. Provide support for medium independent data link functions. Uses the MAC sublayer to provide services to the network layer. LLC1 is for a connectionless link, and LLC2 is for connection-oriented. (ISO 8802/2).

Logical Channel

In X.25 single physical channel between DTE and DCE can be multiplexed to allow a number of virtual calls to take place concurrently.

MAC

Medium Access Control; a sublayer comprising part of the data link and/or physical layers that supports topology-dependent functions (ie dependent upon the type of LAN) and uses the services of the physical layer to provide services to the logical link control sublayer.

MAP

Manufacturing Automation Protocol; originally initiated by General Motors in order to force suppliers to adhere to a prescribed set of OSI-based standards.

Medium The physical component of a network that interlinks devices and provides the pathway over which data can be conveyed. Examples include coaxial cable and optical cable.

MHS Message Handling Service; a general term for the application layer standards being defined by X.400.

MOTIS Message Oriented Text Interchange Systems; a set of text handling standards under development by ISO, with a greater scope than X.400. (DP 8505.2, DP 8883, DP 9065, DP 9066.)

MTA Message Transfer Agent; system responsible for storage and delivery of messages in MHS.

Multiplexing The carrying of more than one data stream over the same connection (apparently) simultaneously.

NBS The US National Bureau of Standards; organises workshops on OSI and OSINET.

Network A collection of equipment and/or transmission facilities for communication between computer systems (whether a single dedicated link, line, dial-up PSTN (telephone) line, public or private data network (PDN), satellite link, etc) more correctly in the OSI context used to define the achievement of end-to-end communication between *end systems,* however accomplished.

Network Architectures
A generic term for the layered approach which individual vendors take towards development of their communications and applications products. Examples include IBM and SNA, DEC and DNA, Honeywell and DSA, and ICL and IPA.

Network Layer
Level 3 of the OSI model. It is the means of establishing connections across a network such that it then becomes possible for transport entities to communicate.

Node
A focal point within a network at which information about a network entity is considered to be located.

NSAP
Network Service Access Point; the service access point which allows entities within network and transport layers to interact. It is situated upon the network layer boundary. It is located by its address which is the subject of ISO 8348/ADD2.

OSA
Open-Systems Architecture; a network architecture standard developed by ISO.

OSCRL
Operating System Command Response Language; OSI group investigating a common job control language.

OSI
Open Systems Interconnection; a term which is used to describe the area of

work concerned with vendor independent standardisation, largely carried
out under the guidance of ISO.

OSI Gateway

A method of providing access to an
OSI network from a non-OSI system
by mapping the sets of protocols
together.

OSI Reference Model

Seven layer model defined by an ISO
subcommittee as a framework around
which an Open Systems Architecture
can be built. It describes the concep-
tual structure of systems which are to
communicate.

OSINET

An OSI demonstration network
organised by NBS in the United
States.

OTSS

Open Systems Transport and Session
Support; IBM mainframe software
providing OSI transport and session
services.

P1, P2, P3, P7

Different classes of protocol specified
within the CCITT X.400 (MHS)
standards.

Packet-switching

A type of data network based upon
the CCITT X.25 recommendation,
whereby a 'virtual call' is established,
but individual data 'packets' may be
routed across separate physical links
through the network.

PAD

Packet Assembler/Disassembler; con-
verts data at a terminal into 'packets'
(discrete quantities) for transmission
over a communications line and sets

up and addresses calls to another PAD (or system with equivalent functionality). It permits terminals which cannot otherwise connect directly to a packet switched network to access such networks.

PCI

Protocol Control Information; control information passed between peer entities to coordinate the transfer of user data. It is added to the Service Data Unit to create a Protocol Data Unit.

PDU

Protocol Data Unit; created at a given layer in the stack by taking the service data unit from the layer above and adding PCI. This is the information which is passed to the peer entity.

Peer Entity

Active element within an OSI layer which corresponds to an equivalent element in the corresponding layer of a different end system.

Physical Layer

This is the first level of the OSI Reference Model, responsible for transmitting bit streams between data link entities across physical connections.

Presentation Layer

Level 6 in the model; responsible for agreement on how information is represented.

Protocol

A set of rules for the interaction of two or more parties engaged in data transmission or communication. In OSI terms interaction between two layers of the same status in different systems.

Protocol Stack   The set of OSI protocols at all 7 layers required for a particular function or implemented in a particular system.

PSDN   Public Switched Data Network; CCITT term for public packet switched network.

PSE   Packet Switched Exchange; a switching computer which adheres to X.25 packet-level procedures.

PSTN   Public Switching Telephone Network.

PTT   National postal, telephone and telegraphy organisation.

Relay   A term used for a system which performs an intermediate function in the communication between two or more *end systems* (eg a node in a public switched network).

Routeing   Function within a layer to translate title or address of an entity into a path through which the entity can be reached.

ROSE   Research Open Systems for Europe.

SAP   Service Access Point; allows entities within adjacent layers to interact (see NSAP).

SASE   Specific Application Service Elements; those parts of the OSI Application Layer which include FTAM, JTM, VT and MOTIS.

SC	Subcommittee; within ISO, SC21 has responsibility for development of standards for OSI layers 5 to 7, SC6 for layers 1 to 4, SC18 for message handling systems.
SDF	Simple Document Formattable; the most basic structure for text interchange.
SDU	Service Data Unit; the unit which is passed from the layer above, when combined with the PCI it forms that layer's PDU.
Segmenting	A function to map one SDU into multiple PDUs.
Service	The interface between a layer and the next higher layer (in the same system), ie the features of that layer (and below) which are available for selection and the conditions reported.
Service Primitive	The elements defined in one type of ISO OSI standard which specify in a precise manner the services provided by a particular layer.
Session	A period during which a connection exists between two points in a network such that data and/or commands may be exchanged.
Session Layer	Fifth layer in the model, responsible for managing and coordinating the dialogue between end systems.
Slotted Ring	One of the types of local area network, specified in DP 8802/6 and by

a British Standard; Cambridge Ring is an example.

SNA

IBM's proprietary Systems Network Architecture, which is layered but at present has only some architectural similarity to OSI.

SNACP

SubNetwork Access-Protocol; the lowest sublayer of the network layer, X.25 is an example of an SNACP. It provides a service to the next sublayer.

SNDCP

SubNetwork Dependent Convergence Protocol; this sublayer maps a consistent standardised service onto the service provided by the subnetwork.

SNICP

SubNetwork Independent Convergence Protocol; this sublayer provided the network service to the transport layer (only two SNICPs are required − one for connectionless and one for connection-oriented service).

SPAG

Standards Promotion and Application Group − a consortium of European suppliers developing functional standards.

Sublayer

A group of functions in a layer. A sublayer can be null if there is no function to perform.

Subnetwork

The more correct term in the OSI context for a physical network which may in fact be only one in a series of such physical networks which links two or more *end systems.*

TC	Technical Committee; within ISO, TC97 has responsibility for SC6, SC18 and SC21, which are the primary sub-committees developing OSI standards.
Teletex	An international service for document interchange, which provides rapid exchange of text via the telephone network and other public data networks. Unlike telex, teletex is a method rather than a specific network or system (CCITT F.200, T.60, T.61 and T.62).
Token Bus	One of the types of local area network, specified in ISO 8802/4 and IEEE 802.4.
Token Passing	A class of local area network using a 'token' − data and protocol information in a standard format − as the means of moving messages between devices. Only the device holding a 'token' may pass messages.
Token Ring	One of the types of local network, specified in ISO 8802/5 and IEEE 802.5; the type of LAN given primary support by IBM. This type of LAN employs a system of token passing.
TOP	Technical and Office Protocols; a set of functional standards designed for the office environment, initiated by Boeing in the US.
Transport Classes	The method by which the options of the transport layer are grouped into five subsets.

Transport Layer   Fourth level of the Reference Model, charged with guaranteeing end-to-end communication between end systems.

Triple X   The CCITT recommendations X.3, X.28 and X.29 — which jointly define standards for asynchronous terminals to access a mainframe (or X.25 packet terminal) via a PAD.

UA   User Agent; within MHS, the system responsible for originating and receiving messages.

Virtual Circuit   A logical transmission path through an X.25 packet switched network established by the exchange of set-up messages between two DTEs. The circuit may use more than one physical circuit, or share a physical circuit with other virtual circuits.

VTP   Virtual Terminal Protocol, one of the protocols being developed for the OSI application layer for standard terminal access to computer systems (DP9040 and DP9041).

WAN   A Wide Area Network; makes use of communications facilities which can carry data to remote sites, could be a public data network (PDN) such as BT's PSS or a private network.

X.3, X.28, X.29   The set of Triple-X protocols.

X.21   The CCITT Recommendation defining interfaces for synchronous transmission over Public Data Networks (*circuit-switched* networks).

X.25   The CCITT Recommendation defin-
                                ing interfaces to packet-mode ter-
                                minals on packet-switched networks,
                                as used by British Telecom's PSS and
                                many other national and private
                                networks.

X.25 (1980), X.25 (1984)   The variants of X.25 agreed by
                                CCITT at its plenary meetings in 1980
                                and 1984, respectively. The 1980 ver-
                                sion is a subset of the 1984 version.

X.400   The CCITT series of Message Handl-
                                ing Service Recommendations for text
                                interchange which will precede, but be
                                similar to, the final ISO standards
                                (MOTIS) for message handling and
                                document interchange.

X-OPEN   A European venture between
                                manufacturers outside the bounds of
                                the OSI model, to create software por-
                                tability between a variety of computer
                                systems.

Appendix 2

MAP and TOP Specification Summary for Version 3.0

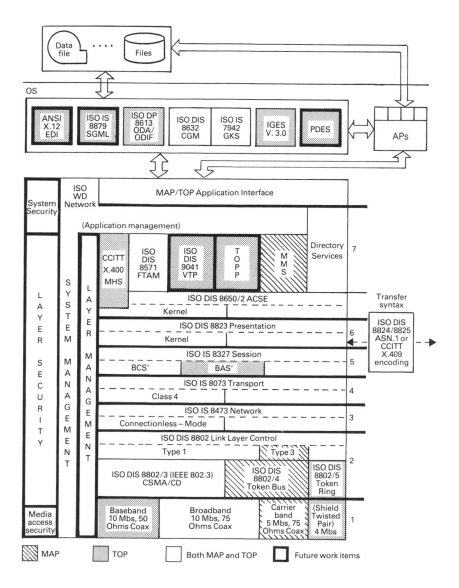

Appendix 3

Relevant MAP Organisations

ISO
International Organisation of Standardisation
Central Secretariat
1 Rue de Varembe
CH-1211
Genève
Switzerland

MAP
European MAP Users Group
Building 30
Cranfield Institute of Technology
Cranfield
Bedfordshire
MK43 0AL
England

General Motors Corporation
Manufacturing Engineering and Development
Advanced Product and Manufacturing Engineering Staff
(APMES)
APMES A/MD-39
GM Technical Center
Warren
MI 48090-9040
USA

Society of Manufacturing Engineers
One SME Drive
PO Box 930
Dearborn
Michigan
48121
USA

Other Organisations
British Standards Institution
2 Park Street
London
W1A 2BS
England

CCITT
International Telecommunication Union
Place des Nations
CH-1211
Genève 20
Switzerland

IEEE Standards Office
345 East 47th Street
New York
NY 10017
USA

National Bureau of Standards
Building 225
Room B218
Caitherburg MD 20899
USA

Index